LITERACY ACTIVITIES
for Small Groups

Liz Simon

ELEANOR CURTAIN
PUBLISHING

First published in 1999

Eleanor Curtain Publishing
906 Malvern Road
Armadale Vic 3143
Australia

National Library of Australia
Cataloguing-in-Publication entry:

Simon, Liz.
Literacy activities for small groups

ISBN 1 875327 54 1

1. Reading (Primary). 2. Active learning. I. Title.

372.41/62

Production by Publishing Solutions
Edited by Ruth Siems
Designed by David Constable
Illustrated by Marjory Gardner
Printed in Australia

Contents

Acknowledgments

I want to sincerely thank Shirley Bickler, a Reading Recovery tutor who led the Literacy Initiative for Teachers (LIFT) project in the Westminster Local Education Authority, London. She assisted classroom teachers to implement an hour-long reading program, first developed in New Zealand. Shirley, with the help of New Zealand teachers Raewyn Hickey and Tracey Sutherland, convinced me of the importance of text-based, pre-planned focused teaching in the classroom.

I would also like to acknowledge Cheryl Evans (Head Teacher, St Luke's CE Primary School, Queens Park, London) for her wonderful terms 'cottoning on', 'taking off' and 'flying high'. Thank you to two South Australian teachers, Alicia Simon who contributed her experience, working with CD-ROM Living books and Ann Stewart who forwarded her work using Edward De Bono's Six thinking hats. Also, I want to extend my gratitude to Jeff Wait (principal of Clovelly Primary School, Adelaide) for his understanding and assistance.

I would have been lost without Eleanor Curtain's perceptive and knowledgable advice.

This book is dedicated to all the children who have said 'Ohhhh! I want to do our reading group' and 'I love the reading activity time.'

Introduction

If only classroom populations were homogenous groupings! But the actual state of most (if not all) classroom populations is that each child's literacy development and learning needs are different.

The material presented in this book is especially for teachers who want to manage a differentiated literacy program, and who want more focused learning for children in their early years at school.

Managing a reading program where teachers work with small groups – such as when involved in guided reading – while the rest of the class is involved in literacy activities is challenging. How to organise your classroom, how to begin to set children on the path of independent learning, and what activities to select so that children discover ways of learning and develop specific literacy understandings and knowledge are a few of the issues you have to deal with.

1 In the classroom

Teaching practices

Fostering individual children's literacy development requires management and teaching practices which allow you to work, uninterrupted, with small reading groups. These practices involve:

- using text as the stimulus for focused teaching
- providing relevant literacy activities
- gradually introducing new learning
- using a management task board
- having support strategies
- undertaking relevant assessment

Using text as the stimulus for focused teaching

After shared reading, the learning focus is reinforced during literacy activity.

During shared and guided reading, children learn to recognise and understand text in the context of its use. Texts such as big books, poems, story books and CDs are used to plan teaching focuses, which means that you have in mind during a lesson or series of lessons a specific understanding, a piece of knowledge and/or a learning strategy that children will be directed towards. In this way, the teacher and the children are working at all times to a purposeful plan. This focused learning is then reinforced during the literacy activity component of the reading program.

Semantic and language learning should happen as text is explored. The study of meaning in language (semantics) is always central to story orientation and reading. This involves the **storyline,** for example, characters, events; **predicting** what might happen, what could happen, what happens next; **retelling**; and **analysis**.

The study of sentence structure (syntax) and words (morphology and phonology) are specially selected as teaching focuses. Examples of language focuses are listed below:

Print:
- locating print on the page (rather than illustrations)
- locating where to start to read – left-right directionality
- reading left page before right
- spacing between words
- one-to-one matching

Language features:
- identifying first or last letter of a word, noting the term 'word'
- identifying upper- and lower-case letters, identifying and using the term 'capital letter'
- identifying capitals at the beginning of names and sentences
- identifying high-frequency words and words beginning with a given letter
- identifying sentence structure and punctuation – sentence stops, question and answer, direct speech and quotation marks, speech bubbles, interjections and exclamation marks, commas, apostrophes for contractions and possessive
- identifying vowels
- identifying conjunctions (eg *and, or* and *but*)
- dividing words into syllables, compound words, words within words
- identifying root words and word endings
- searching for spelling patterns or rhyming words
- identifying digraphs, consonant blends
- learning to identify nouns, proper nouns, pronouns, adjectives, verbs and adverbs
- identifying antonyms and synonyms
- identifying singular and plural

- developing a knowledge of English language forms, for example, she/he, her/his, they/their
- identifying verb tenses

Focuses could also include knowledge about non-fiction books:
- reading for information
- looking for key words, summarising
- using a glossary, index and contents
- becoming familiar with scientific and technical language

Providing relevant literacy activities

Guided reading happens while the rest of the class is involved in literacy activity.

The literacy activities that different groups of children will engage in while you work with small reading groups need to be relevant and carefully selected. The purpose of literacy games and activities is to allow children to build on knowledge imparted during focused learning and discover new concepts through active exploration and experimentation. Careful selection of activities means that:
- the activities reinforce particular learning focuses
- children, after being shown how to use the activities, can manage them independently without teacher intervention
- the 'hands-on' emphasis allows children to manipulate, reuse and discover knowledge, understandings and ways of learning
- the activities can be revisited by new and delayed learners

The activities must be appropriate to the level of reading development, and meet each child's learning needs.

Emergent activities ('cottoning on') are for the emergent reader who is retelling and sequencing ideas in stories, and independently reading simple repetitive text. At the same time, this reader is learning to recognise, write and understand the significance of letters and sounds. Also, this reader is realising that stories are structured and that sentences are comprised of words, spacing, phrasing and punctuation (full stop).

At the **early level** ('taking off'), a broader range of reading genres are experienced and the reader is explicitly encouraged to read fluently to maintain meaning – to 'read as you talk'.

Giving reasons why they like certain stories or parts of stories shows that the reader is beginning to move towards early analytical thinking. Word vocabulary and knowledge about punctuation is steadily growing.

Fluent readers ('flying hight') are quite independent and are now interacting more with texts and reading a variety of genres. This reader is no longer absorbed with decoding, but is interpreting, inferring and thinking more critically about texts. Word study is extended by examining word and sentence structures (grammar) and word meanings. They now know most punctuation forms.

Gradually introducing new learning

Whenever you are introducing new learning, think in terms of building blocks. One block is put down, then another added, and another added on top of that. Children feel secure when they begin with something they know and that is then linked to something new.

Using a management task board

The management task board guides children through activities they know and can manage. You plan a series of activities for each group which children systematically follow, and they move from the first activity to the next at their own pace. Note that not all children will finish all the tasks listed for their group.

The task board allows you to manage differentiated learning, and is the first step towards children becoming independent and responsible learners by making them responsible for the organisation of their own learning.

Have cards that denote activities and Blu-tack them on the board giving each group no more than four relevant activities. Change the cards daily or weekly. You can state 'Read 5 poems', or 'Read 3 big books', and they can choose which poems or books they want to read. You can have a mixture of learning centres or activity collection areas for the different groups to go to.

A management task board, when fully operational, can look like this:

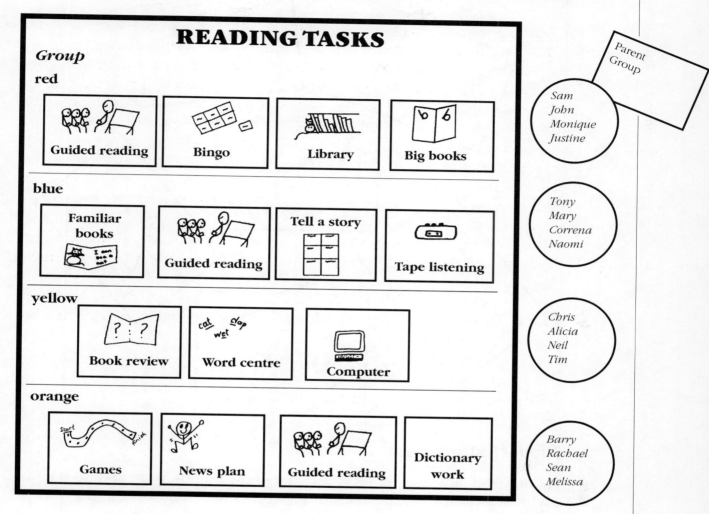

Five-year-old children can learn to use a task board. When they first begin school, allow them some time to settle into a school routine then gradually teach them how to use the task board. Write a specific task on the card, for example: 'abc game' (you may also want to adopt this more supportive approach with children unfamiliar with task boards).

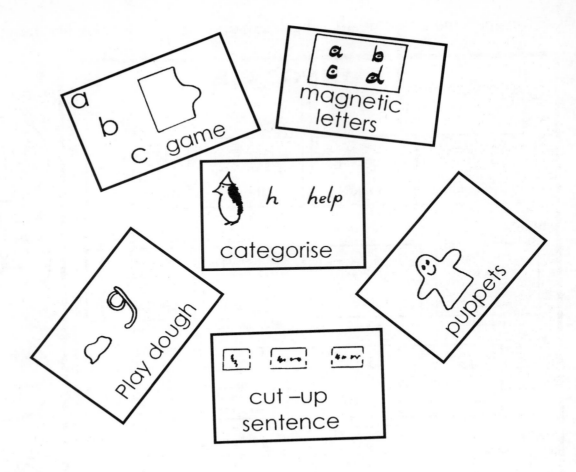

Support strategies

Children will always feel secure if they know that they are able to control any activity before it becomes an independent activity. The buzz of confident children in the classroom, managing their own learning, occurs when certain teaching support strategies are used:

- ensuring the learning focus is made clear. For example, during repeated readings of the text the same focus is reinforced in different ways.
- class circles, where games and activities are played and demonstrated before the children are expected to use the games and activities
- management procedures being modelled and purposefully practised before children are expected to use the procedures. For example, children practise using the management task board before they are expected to use it independently.

Assessment and grouping

Children are grouped for guided reading according to ability. Assessment of letter and/or word knowledge and reading behaviour (running records – miscue analysis) determines groupings. These groups are generally no more than 6 children, and either work independently or interdependently on carefully selected activities that are differentiated and meet each group's learning needs.

For this group, the focus of learning is high-frequency words. During the book introduction and guided reading, the teacher decides which word would be suitable to reinforce during literacy activity.

Learning centres and activity collection areas

Managing literacy activity – the set time independent involvement takes place – is made easier if there are a limited number of learning centres and/or areas where literacy activities are kept. Variety is maintained by continually adding new activities to the centres or areas. Colour coding each activity for a specific group's use allows the children to make choices that suit their level of development.

Alphabet centre

Have a variety of alphabet books, games and activities for the children to choose from, for example, alphabet jigsaws, grids, matching pictures and letters, matching upper- and lower-case letters, large letters written on laminated cardboard. Provide a sand tray, playdough, small blackboards, chalk, paper, pens.

Word centre

As you work on aspects of language features during shared reading – for example, 2-letter consonant blends, digraphs, suffixes, rhyming words, antonyms, synonyms, spelling patterns (eg *-ut, -ough*) – place activities that reinforce the learning in the word centre. Provide magnetic letters so children can make and remake words and store cards in video cases.

Big books

Gradually add to the big book section each week. When you have built the numbers to 6–8 big books, state a limit the children must read, for example: 'Read at least 3 big books'. The children will know the story very well after a week of focusing on a particular learning aspect and reading and retelling the story each day.

Give children a magnifying glass to be 'story detectives' and find particular initial letters or words after they have read the text.

Library

Library books could follow a theme, for example, 'giants'. A thinking question could be attached to the library stand, for example: 'Are all giants in stories bad?'

Library books on a book stand with cushions nearby give the children a comfortable area to read their favourite book. It would be a very uninspiring reading program if only books used in shared and guided reading were read.

Reading library books allows beginning readers to practise handling books, turning pages and 'reading' the pictures. More competent readers will be using what they have learned in a more independent way. Children love to look at and read books with imaginative storylines, rich language and creative pictures of characters and places. Their appreciation of books is further enhanced by reading library books.

Taped stories, poems, songs

Make or collect taped stories for children to read along to. This is an excellent way to help some children learn to read more confidently. A wonderful experience is to tape individual children singing songs, and then write the songs on card or in a book and have children sing along as they listen to the tape.

Games

A variety of language games are colour coded for different groups to use.

Place the games in a particular area. You may need a rod to hang board games on. Place Bingo games in a tray. Provide counters, dice, pegs and any other equipment associated with games.

Books we know

Books that are read in guided reading groups are placed in 'books we know' boxes. Each group has its own box. You can then ask children to

'Read 4 familiar stories'. It is also stimulating for children if you have, say, fluffy animals or puppets for them to read their familiar stories to.

Rhymes and short poems

Ask the children to read five poems during the literacy activity.

As well as reading big books, read lots of rhymes and catchy poems written in large print. These can be used when planning language learning focuses: for example, 'Jack and Jill' has many high-frequency words to concentrate on.

Store familiar rhymes and poems in an area where the children can easily access them. Set a limit, such as: 'Read 5 rhymes'. You can vary how poems are read, for example by having missing words to insert.

Writing

It is not enough for children to learn about literacy structures, language conventions and punctuation by experiencing reading activities only. Many of the strategies, understandings and knowledge children need for reading are replicated during writing.

Writing done during literacy activity should not be seen as the complete writing program, but a time to reinforce and further discover through experimentation what has been learned during more focused reading and writing lessons.

Set up a writing centre if you have the space; otherwise place writing materials in a box: for example, different coloured paper, card, pens, ruler, stamps, books, pictures.

Problem centre

A group of children verbally create stories using pictures of characters and settings, and beginning and ending phrases.

In this centre, place every activity relating to text meaning and sentence structure. For example 'Make a story' – a board covered in felt with felt characters from fairy tales or nursery rhymes with Velcro strips glued on the back of the figures. Puppets to retell stories can also be kept in this centre.

Also place activities that reinforce learning about word order, spacing, capital letter use, punctuation and grammar. Children can be instructed to 'Do 5 activities in the problem centre'.

Read around the room

Use the displays of artwork and information in the classroom for children to reread during literacy activity. This allows children to revisit information about topics studied after the topic is completed. Also, vary how innovated stories are presented – some in big-book form, but others displayed around a wall so children can easily read them.

Getting started

The example of management shown here is directed at 5-year-olds (after six months at school), and 6- to 8-year-olds who have not experienced using a management task board, literacy activities, or small focused reading groups. Children who have experienced these management practices will probably need less time and effort learning the required procedures. Although, the gradual introduction of independent learning and activities begins in the first week of the school year, the procedures could be put into practice any time during the year.

You need to first think about the type of behaviour needed when children take responsibility for their own learning. Consider these points when setting rules for literacy activity:

- on completion of an activity and after packing away the material, the children move to the next task
- there is the explicitly stated expectation that children do not interrupt when you are working with a group
- use a chart that caters for toileting needs
- the children have 'reading' books and there is a finished work basket for children to place work in for you to see

It will take at least 4–6 weeks to establish literacy activity (approx. 35 minutes each day) in the classroom. Introduce the activities gradually during shared reading or in class circles. You will need games and activities which reinforce a literacy learning focus and need minimum supervision.

Week 1	Big book, plan a teaching focus 3 rhymes (you can begin assessing children)
Week 2	Big book, plan a teaching focus 2–3 new rhymes demonstrate 4 games or activities – vary the complexity, so each group has an activity or game to do Introduce management task board – 2 activities for each group
Week 3	Big book or poem Activity from planned teaching focus Using management task board – 2 activities for each group Introduce library and tape activities Work with one guided reading group
Week 4	Big book or poem Activity from planned teaching focus Using management task board Work with two guided reading groups

Be prepared to stop literacy activity at any time to revise rules, practise appropriate behaviour, read the task board, and practise the collection and putting away of activities and associated equipment.

Begin weeks 1 and 2

Introduce one big book in week one and another in week two. Set teaching focuses, for example, letter knowledge or high-frequency words.

During weeks 1 and 2 the children read and chant rhymes for example 'Jack and Jill', 'Humpty Dumpty', 'Twinkle, Twinkle Little Star'. This will later be a literacy activity ('Read 3 to 10 rhymes'). Write the rhymes in big print and have children read them each day. More experienced readers can begin by reading poems.

You may in week 1 and certainly in week 2, begin to assess the children's letter and word knowledge and take running records to determine reading strategies used.

During week 2, children will also be learning games and activities as a way of establishing tasks for literacy activity.

Week 2, Day 1

Board game: Children move along numbered coloured spots on a board and follow instructions written on cards (fluent readers).

Sit with the children in a circle on the floor. Choose three children to participate in the board game where they move along a path from 'start' to 'finish' and read instructions. Show children how to throw the dice on the board. Each child throws and the highest score determines the first person to begin.

Demonstrate the whole game, and try to include the spectators by asking 'What do you think it will land on? 'What will the next number be?'

Let the players read their own instructions and move their own counters.

Play a second time, with three new players.

Place the game on a table and choose four players from the demonstration groups to play it. Put paper and pens on the other tables for the rest of the children to draw their favourite part from the big book. Allow about 10 minutes for literacy activity.

Day 2

Put the game from Day 1 out on a table and after another demonstration, a group of 4 children can play it. Put paper and pencils for general writing on a number of tables, leaving two tables free for the 'making words' activity and a Bingo game. Begin to instil in the children the need to complete their task and put away their materials.

Demonstrate two new games in a class circle. Game 1 one is a quick game and game 2 will involve one or two groups of 6.

Game 1: Making words (emergent or early readers)

From the big books and rhymes or poems read in weeks 1 and 2, focus on some high-frequency words: for example *the, and, is, went.*

On a space on the floor, put out magnetic letters and cards with these words written on them. Children can practise placing the letters on or underneath the words. Put out only the letters they will need.

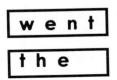

Game 2: Bingo (emergent or early readers)

From the big books and rhymes or poems read in weeks 1 and 2, focus on certain letters, and high-frequency words or phrases. Make letter or high-frequency word or short phrase bingo boards and cards. Have 6 different coloured counters prepared for each player. Choose 6 children to demonstrate the game to the class. You may want to demonstrate bingo with a second group of six.

Place the two new games on tables and allow 10–15 minutes for literacy activity.

Day 3

Put out the board game, bingo, magnetic letters and words, rhymes, big books and writing materials.

Game: Categorising

Have thick card board 30 cm x 56 cm (approximately). Write categorising headings on the top. Make pockets by taping frieze tape across the board, leaving approximately 10 cm space between each tape length. Make appropriate pictures for children to place under the headings. The example shown has toys, animals, people and machines. You may want to use other headings to complement a story or topic you are beginning to study in the classroom.

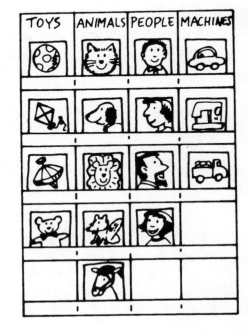

Day 4

Set up tables, with board games, bingo and magnetic letters and words, rhymes, big books, and writing materials. By week 2, day 4 there should be two activities for each group.

Children should be roughly assessed by now. Put the children into groups and give each group a colour code.

Introduce the management task board where the different groups will be given a different sequence of two games or activities. Include a card with a symbol to indicate working with the teacher. The reading task board may look like this:

Groups	READING TASKS	
blue	rhymes	board game (from day 1)
red	big book	magnetic letters
yellow	Bingo	writing
orange	board game	categorising

Read the tasks with the children and indicate the tables with the first set of tasks.

Get each group to go to the table where their first tasks are placed. Show them where their tasks are stored. Get the groups to put their first tasks away, take them out and put them away again. You may want to do this a few times.

Children sit on the floor while you put the second tasks out on the tables. The groups go to the table where their second tasks are, put them away, take them out and put them away again.

Read the task board again and have groups collect and do their tasks.

Have literacy activity for 15–20 minutes, with the children putting their games and activities away as they complete them.

Although group work (guided reading) does not begin this week, sit with a group for 10 minutes of interruption-free time. Have an activity which enables you to monitor the groups, for example, making plasticine letters.

Day 5

Begin by reading the task board and reminding the children where the games and activities are stored. Today the groups collect their tasks, complete them and move on to the next task.

While the children are settled doing their games and activities, try to distance yourself and observe how they work together, and anything that is causing a blip in the smooth running of the reading tasks

After literacy activity has finished (approximately 20 minutes) get the children to sit on the floor and ask each group, one at a time, to go and check their replacement of games and activities. Also, ask three or four children what they have learnt during literacy activity.

Demonstrate a new game: Alphabet Spin (emergent readers – see page 34).

Demonstrate the game to the whole class. Play the game with a group of four children. You may not want to play it to its conclusion.

Week 3

Introduce a new big book for the week, emphasise your teaching focus and have a follow-up activity that relates to a group's learning needs.

Choose children to model the collection and placement of games, activities, equipment, where to go to the big books and rhymes, and the tidying up after using an activity and moving on to the next activity. Also, model how the children return to the board when they don't know what to do next.

Read the task board and have children collect the tasks from areas or go to the centres. At the beginning of the week, distance yourself and observe how the children are managing (by doing this the children are getting used to you not being amongst them).

Sometime this week set three tasks for each group, with additional activities like library and tape listening.

Towards the end of this week, you begin to work with small guided reading groups. Initially, work with one group for 10 minutes. Remind the children about 'working procedures' especially allowing the teacher to work uninterrupted with reading groups. Leave time to rove, at the beginning when settling the children, during the session and at the end of the session. This will allow children to tell you about any problems they may be having.

Week 4

Introduce a new big book or a poem written in large print. Introduce a new game or activity generated from the teaching focus. Try to work with two guided reading groups this week.

Weeks 5 and 6

Continue shared reading and literacy activity, introducing a new activity each week (generated from shared reading teaching focus). By the end of the sixth week there should be four tasks for each group, with literacy activity being approximately 35 minutes duration, and you should be working with three guided reading groups.

Some suggested resources

- management task board
- magnetic letters
- storage containers
- taped stories
- CD-ROMs
- books of rhymes, poems, wordless text
- alphabet books
- dictionaries
- puppets, felt boards and figures
- grids and column-boards
- commercial alphabet puzzles, eg matching letters and jigsaws
- commercial word puzzles, eg consonant blends, compound words, word building, silent consonant, irregular plurals, rhyming words, homophones, synonyms, antonyms
- varied sentence-building kits (commercial)

2 Cottoning on

Activities for emergent readers

Activities stressing meaning

Sequencing cards

Focus: *ordering the ideas in stories*

Read a fairy tale to the children, for example *The Three Pigs*. Follow up with a class circle where children demonstrate how to sequence pictures. (Frank Schaffer's fairy tale sequencing cards are a wonderful resource for this.) As a literacy activity, children begin sequencing three picture cards and retell the tale. Later, increase it to four cards and then give them the complete set (six).

As children become more experienced at sequencing ideas, photocopy three or four pictures from the big book you are reading and have children put the pictures in order. They can retell the story to each other using the pictures as a guide.

For example, the story *Goodnight, Goodnight* begins with the character reading and imagining fairy tale characters visiting. In the first picture her light is on over the bed, indicating night-time. In the last picture the light is off, indicating morning. Children need to perceive the time change indicators in these pictures.

Draw a favourite character

Focus: *reinforcing knowledge about characterisation in stories*

Children draw a favourite character from a story they know.

This is _____

Wordless texts

Focus: *children using picture cues to create stories*

At one time, series such as Reading 360, Sunshine, Eureka and others included picture books without accompanying text. These resources are often left neglected in the resource room. During shared reading, teach the children how to create stories from the pictures in these books.

Once children know how to use them, set this as a literacy activity: 'Tell a story'.

Early book report

Focus: *knowing the first and last part of a story*

As a focus during shared reading, ask children what comes first and what comes last in the story. You may have to teach some children the concepts of first and last. You can do this when they line up and/or you can manipulate different coloured counters on card: Which colour is first? Which colour is last?

During literacy activity, children can do a very simple book report by drawing the first (beginning) and then the last (ending) part of story.

The big enormous turnip

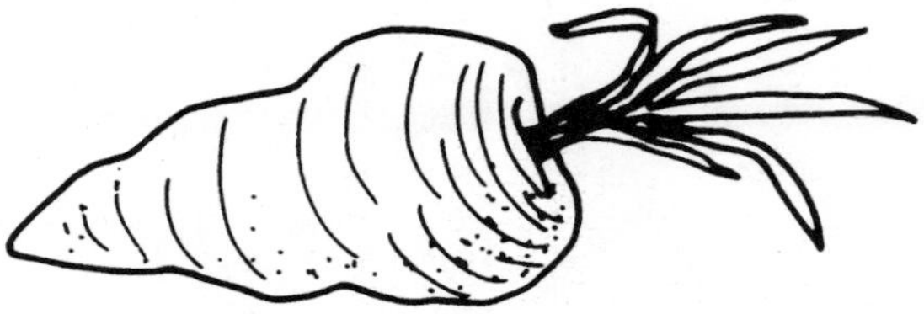

first

last

Stick puppets

Focus: *reading parts of a text*

Make stick puppets of characters from stories like *I Know an Old Lady Who Swallowed a Fly*. During literacy activity, the children can use the puppets to either verbally rehearse the repetitive ideas and language from the story or to read cards with phrases from the story.

Retelling

Focus: *reinforcing knowledge and language from stories*

Make felt shape characters, from stories such as *The Three Billy Goats Gruff*. This is a wonderful story because of its repeated ideas, and its language and imaginative aspects.

During literacy activity, the children use felt characters to retell the main parts of a story.

Book making

Focus: *children see how stories are made*
children learn to read by writing

Read a big book which includes a repeated phrase, for example 'I am ...' in *Smarty Pants*. Link the phrase to books children have read during guided reading (from the 'books we know' box). Follow up by taking photographs of each child and modelling the making of an 'I am ...' big book.

During literacy activity, children can make their own books. On each page write 'I am':

> I am .... [name] (if a child cannot write his / her name write it on
> card to be copied)
> I am .... [five]
> I am .... [happy]

Later, choose shared or guided reading material that introduces new phrases (and high-frequency words, for example *on, the, see, he, we, to*. These can later be used to gradually extend the phrases).

Repeat the phrase on each page, changing only the verb or noun at the end of the sentence, for example:

> I can   I went   I like

Activities stressing visual aspects

Letter, word, picture categorising (concepts of print)

Focus: *reinforce the concepts letter, word and picture*

When reading any big book or poem get children to point to the picture, isolate a letter and run their finger around words. Children need to know the concepts and differences between a picture, letter and word.

As a follow-up, use alphabet books which have pictures, letters and words and again get the children to distinguish between the picture, letter and word.

As a literacy activity, a group can categorise letters, words and pictures using a board like the one below. Provide a group of pictures, letters and words taken from known shared and guided reading material and have children place the items in the appropriate columns.

pictures	letters	words
🐱	a b c	I am is

Initial letters

●●●●●●●●●●●●

Focus: *confirming using the initial letter cue*
names begin with a capital

The first week children begin school, make and laminate name cards for each child. Using what the children know, their names, get them to look at the initial (capital) letter as a strategy to help them confirm that what they have read is correct.

During shared reading, each child reads their name (later they read other children's names) and place the name on the 'I am at school today' board. The names must be placed in the matching letter pocket.

This board and the children's names become a group literacy activity. Children match the initial letters and place names in the relevant pockets.

A	B	C Chris	D	G	H
Amelia	Barry	Correna	Davin	Gavin	Harley
J	K				
John	Kia-Lee				

Sequencing letters in names

Focus: *learning to place letters in name in correct sequence*

Write the child's name in large print on card, and give the child a small magnetic board and letters that form their name. The child forms their name and then writes it.

Handwriting

Focus: *learning letters through handwriting*

Write known letters in big print on laminated cards. Children use these as a guide when practising the letters on personal blackboards or making plasticine letters.

Write letters on laminated card and have children either write over them using thin whiteboard markers or tracing paper.

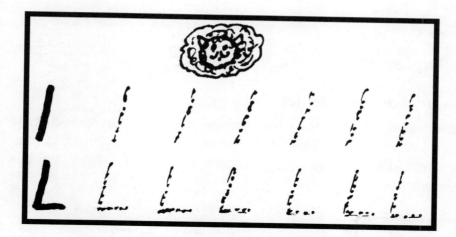

Feely box or bag filled with plastic letters

Focus: *a kinaesthetic approach to learning letters*

Put some plastic letters in a feely box or bag. Children sit in their group and each have a turn putting their hand in the box, feeling a letter, describing it and saying what the letter is.

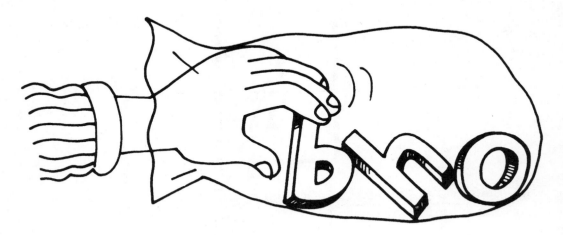

Pegging letters

Focus: *reinforcing letter knowledge*

Write letters known to the children on cards, and provide a variety of pictures or articles to be pegged. Children select a picture and matching initial letter and peg them together. This exercise is also good for manipulative skill development.

Lacing cards

Focus: *matching pictures to letters*
matching letters to letters

Make cards with four to six letters above a line and matching pictures randomly placed below the line. Make a hole above the letter and one below the picture. Tie different coloured shoe laces or round 'spaghetti' plastic strips at the top of the letter. (You could use 'Match pictures/ letters' from Smart Kids, Artamon NSW.)

The children thread and match letter to picture.

Write the letters on the left-hand side of a laminated card and randomly place matching letters on the right-hand side. Make holes in the card and tie the lacing after the letter on the left-hand side. The children thread and match letter to letter.

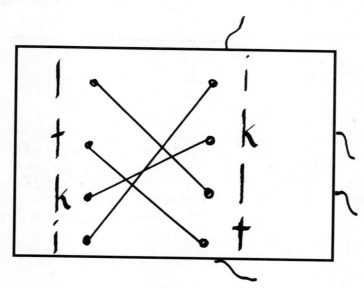

Matching cards: lower case and capital letter

Focus: *reinforcing knowledge, matching capital and lower case letters*

An example of a big book that can be used to model lower case letter and capital match is *Guinea Pig Grass*. The words 'Guinea' and 'Go' using the capital are repeated on most pages while words 'grass', 'gather', 'grow' using the lower case 'g' are repeated in the text.

Guinea pig grass
Where will I gather my guinea pig grass?
Go to the kitchen?
This isn't the place for grass to grow.

Make large cards with capitals and matching lower case letters. Children sort and match known letters.

Later, follow up with a commercial jigsaw (you could use 'Letter Match', Galt Toys, Cheadle, Cheshire, UK) which has the picture, lower case, capital and word on a 3-part jigsaw card. As the children assemble the jigsaw they see on one card the different concepts of letter, word and picture.

Jigsaw letters

. . . .

Focus: *reinforcing letters learned*

Make a set of round laminated cards with a letter and matching picture cut into jigsaw shapes.

Children manipulate only letters they have learned.

Make ducks or other animals that have a picture, and lower and upper case letters on the body. See Blackline Master 1. Cut out a jigsaw shape in the middle of the body. Change the positions of the picture, and lower and upper case letters on each duck.

Sequencing the alphabet

Focus: *reinforcing knowledge of the alphabet*

Draw a caterpillar with 26 segments on cardboard (see Blackline Master 2), or make a grid. Make a set of alphabet letters or use plastic letters. Children place the alphabet, in order, on the caterpillar or the grid.

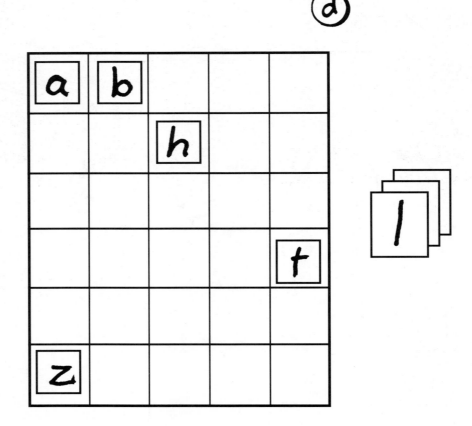

Bingo

· · · · ·

Focus: *reinforcing letter knowledge*

At this level children match lower case to lower case and lower case to capital. Provide about six bingo boards with varied combinations of letters and the complete alphabet on individual cards.

One child is the caller. The rest of the players choose a board and the appropriate number of counters. As the caller says a letter the players place a counter on the letter on their board. If they do not have the letter they miss a turn. At the same time, the caller must place the called letter card face-down under the pile. The first player to cover all the letters on the board wins the game.

Playing bingo reinforces letter knowledge.

Board game – Alphabet spin

Focus: *matching picture with letter*
collaborating, taking turns (social)

Make a game board with pictures around the edge and a spinning disk containing about eight letters in the centre to match the pictures.

Each player spins, says the letter, and places a peg on the matching picture.

Playing alphabet spin.

Activities stressing structure

Early matching of phrases or sentences with pictures

Focus: *how sentences are structured*
reading/matching/ordering/spacing

This is a 3-step developmental matching activity for early readers. When children have secured step 1 they move to step 2, and later to step 3. From shared reading, or as a follow-up from guided reading (for example, PM Starters One: *Me*; Alphakids *Playing, Can You See Me?*).

For step 1, make approximately five matching 'I am ...' sentences. Children place a sentence face up, and then find the matching sentence. They continue until all the sentences are paired.

For step 2, make sentences with a space for the missing word, and provide the missing words on separate cards. Children read the sentence and then place the missing word in the space.

For step 3, make sentences with a matching cut-up and jumbled sentence. Children put the sentence in order, and in most cases finish with a full stop.

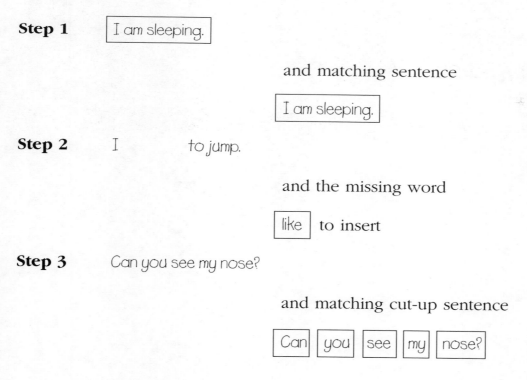

Step 1   I am sleeping.

and matching sentence

I am sleeping.

Step 2   I   to jump.

and the missing word

like to insert

Step 3   Can you see my nose?

and matching cut-up sentence

Can you see my nose?

Phrasing

Focus: *reading phrases as a strategy for fluent reading*

Begin with the rhyme 'Humpty Dumpty'. Write the rhyme and matching phrases on card. Children match the phrases, placing them on top or alongside the rhyme. They read the phrase as they match.

Humpty Dumpty
Sat on the wall.
Humpty Dumpty
Had a great fall.
All the king's horses
And all the king's men
Couldn't put Humpty
Together again.

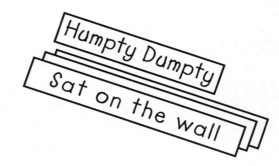

3 Taking off

Activities for early readers

Activities stressing meaning

Days of the week

Focus: *reading and sequencing days of the week*
becoming aware of words within words ... day, sat, sun
names of days begin with capitals

Choose a book that sequences the days of the week (there are many) and as a follow-up, in front of the class in big print on A3 paper, write a child's suggestion for what happens each day. When writing the day, colour the capital in a different colour from the other letters (you could, also, colour the words within the word a different colour).

During literacy activity, a group is given the sheets to paint or draw a picture that matches the message.

On Sunday
I [we] go to
nana's.

On Monday
I [we] go to
the library.

Revealing phrases

Focus: *predicting the next idea*
reading phrases as a strategy for fluent reading (structure)

Don Holdaway, in his book *The Foundations of Learning,* talks about alternative forms of large print, such as using an overhead projector. A story, for example, can be written on an overhead sheet. During shared reading, the story is masked with card and you can 'progressively unmask a text'. After this is done in shared reading, it can become an activity for groups to take turns doing.

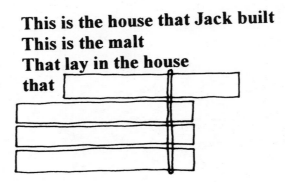

Jigsaw phrases

Focus: *making sense*
reading phrases as a strategy for fluent reading (structure)

Take some catchy poems and write the lines on card, then cut the lines into phrases. children reassemble the lines and read the poem.

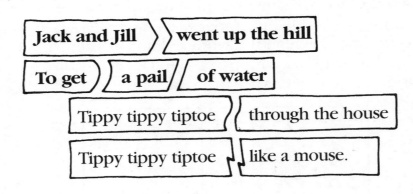

Shape sentences

Focus: *making sense*
reinforcing word vocabulary

During shared reading, read a fairy tale such as *The Little Red Hen*. As a retelling or sequencing exercise, have children recite the answer the different animals give to the hen.

Draw a large hen on A3 paper. Ask children to suggest other answers the animals could give and write a few of these innovations on the hen, for example: 'I will help,' said the cat. 'Yes,' said the pig.

Next, draw card hens and write the innovated direct speech on the hen and phrases indicating direct speech has occurred on separate cards. As a follow-up literacy activity, children can insert the phrases and read the complete sentences.

Make lots more character-shaped cards from other stories where children have to add missing words or phrases.

What am I?

Focus: *predicting from a few selected clues*

There a many books you can use during shared reading that model the 'What am I?' technique. Begin with animals, and later introduce inanimate objects. Children's knowledge about various animals will determine which ones you choose to describe. 'What am I?' cards generally have an accompanying picture hidden somewhere under a flap.

When children learn the pattern of 'What am I?', they can make their own cards during literacy activity.

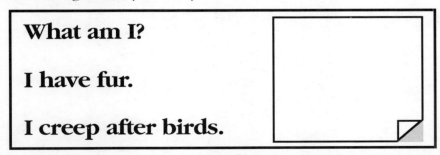

Who am I?

• • • • • • • • • • •

Focus: *predicting from a few selected clues*
characterisation in stories

Use rhymes or big books that you have shared, to model the writing of 'Who am I?' story character cards. For example: 'I am a boy. I fall down a hill.' (Jack from 'Jack and Jill')

Begin the shared session by playing a circle game where a child sits in the middle of the circle with eyes closed while a child from the circle using a disguised voice says, for example: 'Who am I? I have brown eyes and I like to play chasey at playtime.'

Continue the shared session by writing, in front of the children, two or three 'Who am I?' story character examples. Ask the children to choose a well-known character from a book or rhyme, then tell two or three distinctive things about the character.

Who am I?

I have a large boat.

I collect animals two by two

Noah from the Ark

Masks

Focus: *understanding the story and the language*
role play and creating ideas
direct speech in stories (structure)

Children make masks and act out the role of the main character from a story that has been read a number of times. Write a line from the story onto card. For example, use the direct speech of the main character Hush, from the story *Possum Magic* (by Mem Fox). Hush is invisible and she says, 'Grandma, I want to know what I look like?'

Make more masks and accompanying direct speech sentences from other books.

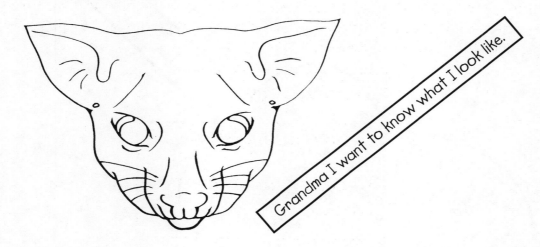

Songs on a guitar

Focus: *reading or singing known songs*

Following the sharing of songs, children can read well-known songs written on A3 card shaped like guitars during literacy activity. Instruct the children to read or sing four songs.

When all the cows were
sleeping
And the sun had gone to bed
Up jumped the scarecrow
And this is what he said
"I'm a dingle dangle
scarecrow with a flippy
floppy hat,
I can shake my hands like
This and shake my feet like
That".

Board games

Focus: *children reading and following instructions*
learning to count on (maths)
taking turns, sharing, appropriate language to each other (social)

If children have not had experience playing board games, begin with a simple version. For example, make this game based on *The Three Little Pigs* (Kate Kitching's Storytime topics). In a class circle, three children can demonstrate how to play the game. They each have a turn throwing the dice, moving around the board and responding to the instructions on the board.

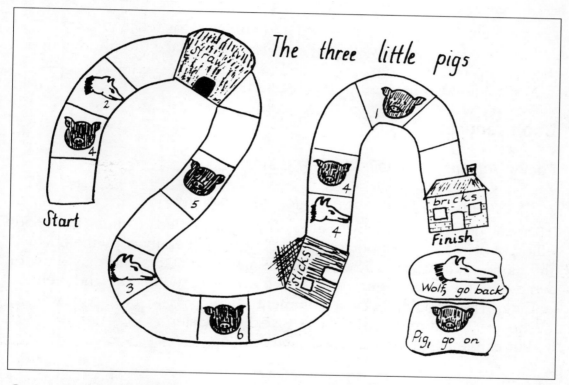

Games with cards that instruct children to 'move on one space', 'go back two', 'miss a turn', with reasons for making these moves such as 'first over the hump' and 'you have a puncture', are appropriate for independent readers. Coloured spots can be used for the path, with stars placed on selected spots. When children land on a star, they take a card and respond to the instruction. Stories from big books and themes that are being followed in the classroom, for example, Space, Christmas, Easter, Winter and Transport, are good sources to direct what learning should come from a board game.

True or false

Focus: *understanding/knowing the story facts*

From shared reading, for example *The Masked Hunter*, write phrases from the text on card:

| The masked hunter becomes a dragonfly. | It eats insects and spiders. |

At the same time write incorrect phrases:

| The masked hunter becomes a caterpillar. | It eats big fish. |

Copy Blackline Master 3 onto card and laminate for reuse.

During literacy activity the children read and place the phrases under the appropriate headings.

You could also have Silly or Sensible boards.

Book reports

Focus: *retelling the main ideas of a story*
giving an opinion
justifying (giving a reason for) the opinion

This can be a literacy activity after shared or guided reading, and modelling of how to write a book report. Children generally copy the title and the name of the author. They draw the main characters and may draw or write how the story begins, one or two events in the middle and then the ending. They could make a comment such as 'The best part was … because …' You may wish to use Blackline Master 4.

Put cards into the children's home reading.

> **I**
> **liked** . . . .
>
> **because** . . . .

Occasionally, vary the presentation of the book report and give a group a character-shaped template. After writing a report on the shape, children can cut around the outline and make either a book or a mobile.

Barrier games

Focus: *children orally describe and instruct*
children listen and respond

Barrier games help to develop oral language and listening skills. A barrier is placed between two children so that one cannot see the other's materials. The 'barrier' can be children sitting back-to-back, a box or a cardboard barrier in the shape of a triangle.

This barrier game is played by two children, one sitting either side of the barrier. Each child has a board with the same pictures around the outside. When demonstrating this game in a class circle, talk about each picture and how the instructor provides as much information as possible: colours, whether it has spots or stripes etc, and the action – monkey hanging from a branch, dog walking, cow looking, bottle tipping, rain dropping and so on.

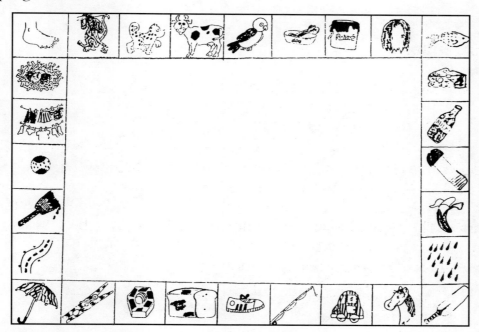

You will need to make two boards divided into boxes around the border. Draw matching pictures in the boxes and/or use pictures from magazines, etc. The boards could be laminated for reuse.

One child instructs while the other child responds:

Instructor: 'Find the pink foot and put a counter on it.'

The child the other side of barrier listens and responds to the instruction.

Instructor: 'Find the brown monkey swinging from a green branch and put a counter on it.'

The child on the other side of the barrier continues to listen and respond.

Read around the room

Focus: *resource for reading a variety of language structures*

Read around the room can be a literacy activity so make your classroom a visual learning centre. Everything displayed in the classroom is a reading resource – wall stories, innovated text, information sheets from a recently studied topic. Also display high-frequency words, topic words, rhyming words.

All the displays arise out of recent activities, where the painting or drawings are done by the children and the writing is done in big print by an adult (a child's writing can still be displayed with an explanation or synopsis written in big print). The displays have a purpose, and children read them as an activity.

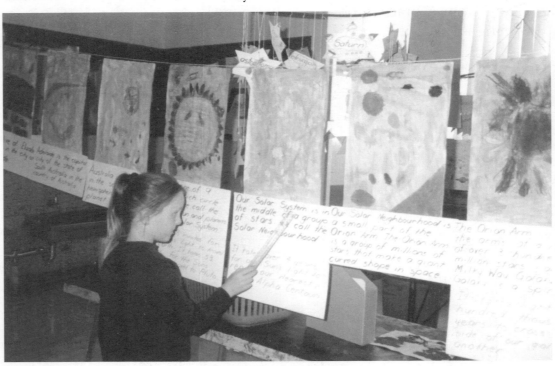

Everything displayed in the classroom is a reading resource.

Some other examples are:
• Reading about classroom features:

> **Through this window**
>
> **I can see the sky.**

- Have photographs with questions:

> What is Sam doing?

> Where is Naomi going?

> Is Gavin saying 'I have an apple' or
> I have a toy car?

- Make a story tree of twisted brown paper or tree branches. Display the whole sequenced story and children's accompanying art work on the tree. The story tree can change stories with the seasons or whatever.

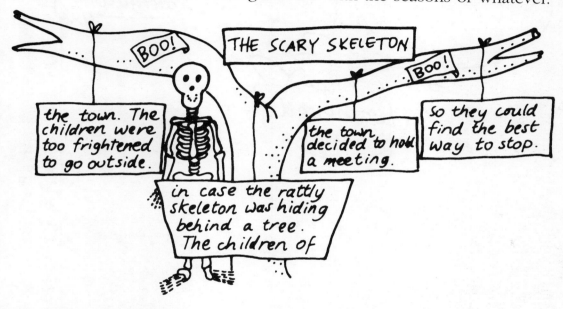

- Hang balloons with phrases or sentences on them.

- Make mobiles of characters and accompanying descriptive words and phrases.

Activities stressing visual aspects

Use big books, poems and words from topics being studied in the class-room to increase the children's word knowledge.

Wall dictionary

Focus: *reinforcing word beginnings (dictionary knowledge)*

Place this activity in the word centre. Write large Aa Bb Cc cards and list words underneath the relevant letter. Begin by listing known words. Leave blank cards for children to write new words to add to the lists. During literacy activity children can read the words and choose one or more to write sentences.

Aa   Bb
apple   ball
an   bat
and   bee

Word chains

Focus: *reinforcing vocabulary*

Make chains of words from fiction or non-fiction texts (this is an appro-priate activity after guided reading). Show children how they find a word they want to learn from the text and write it leaving generous spaces. They fold the paper like a fan after each letter of the word or after each word.

During literacy activity, each child in a particular group finds no more than six words in the text to make word chains.

Rhyming games

Focus: *reinforcing rhyming and spelling patterns*

Lots of books have rhyming patterns. During literacy activity children can reinforce knowledge of rhyming words by playing these games.

Memory game (Concentration)

Make a set of rhyming word cards. Children spread them out face down and take turns to pick up a card. They need to remember where matching rhyming words are. If a child gets a set of two they have another go.

Jigsaws

Make jigsaw words. These jigsaws expose children to rhyming words which sound the same and look the same.

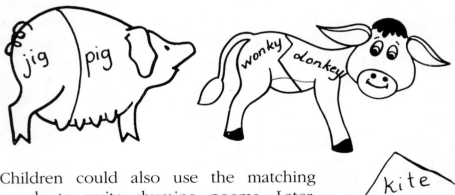

Children could also use the matching words to write rhyming poems. Later, introduce rhyming words that sound the same but look different.

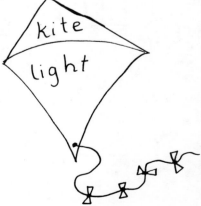

Matching picture or word jigsaws

Focus: *reinforcing digraphs and suffixes*
reinforcing initial consonant blends

You can use different shapes to make digraph, suffix, and initial consonant blend jigsaws. For example, use a tree shape to do 'ee' words, a chicken shape to do 'ch' words, a ring shape to do 'ing' words. Children build the picture jigsaws over the matching word.

Initial consonant blends, suffixes and digraph activities

Focus: *reinforcing initial consonant blends, suffixes, digraphs and spelling patterns*

For these activities, children use a variety of materials to make different words.

Word trees

These 'trees' can be used as a background for different word activities. Label and laminate the tree shape. Children attach word cards with the appropriate blend on the tree with Blu-tack. Store the cards in a video case. This example shows initial consonant blends.

Thread cards

After focusing on a particular word pattern during shared reading, make these cards using heavy A4 cardboard. Make two slits approximately 50 cm wide for the strip card to slide through.

Children read the words as they appear in the window.

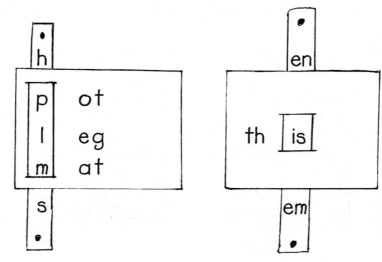

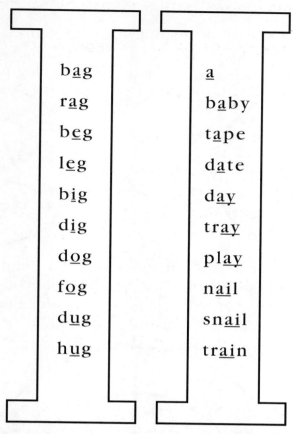

b<u>a</u>g	<u>a</u>
r<u>a</u>g	b<u>a</u>by
b<u>e</u>g	t<u>a</u>pe
l<u>e</u>g	d<u>a</u>te
b<u>i</u>g	d<u>ay</u>
d<u>i</u>g	tr<u>ay</u>
d<u>o</u>g	<u>p</u>l<u>ay</u>
f<u>o</u>g	n<u>ai</u>l
d<u>u</u>g	sn<u>ai</u>l
h<u>u</u>g	tr<u>ai</u>n

For fun, have a face of a character from a big book, and thread words between the eyes or the mouth. The words can follow a pattern, for example short vowels, or the different letter clusters of the long /a/ sound. Again, children read the words as they appear at the window.

Flip books

You can make your own flip books. Smart Kids (Artarmon, NSW) make 'Let's Spell' which includes 3-letter words, start and end blends, and double vowels.

Children flip the page halves backwards and forwards to make and read different words.

Word wheels

Cut a circle approximately 18 cm in diameter from thick cardboard. Make a pointer and loosely fix it with a split pin. On the wheels you could write initial consonants, suffixes, digraphs or spelling patterns.

Another type of word wheel can be made by cutting two circles from thick cardboard. Colour the outer circle a different colour from the inner circle. Loosely fix together with a split pin. An additional focus would be for children to determine which words are sensible.

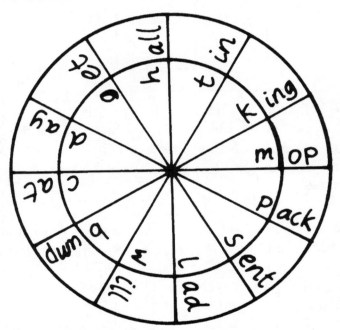

Words within words

Focus: *reinforcing small words within words*
introducing the concept that some words are made up of two or more words
using this knowledge as a reading strategy

Write words on card and give the children a 'window' aid (made from fairly thick card). The children put the window over words they see within a word, and then write the words they see.

this

something

inside

Jigsaw words

Focus: *reinforcing the spelling strategy of breaking longer words into syllables*

Marie Clay, in *Reading Recovery,* says that children begin by 'hearing big chunks of sound'. During shared or guided reading and writing, children become aware of syllables and this knowledge is reinforced during literacy activity.

   Children build the jigsaw, reading the parts of the words and finally the complete word.

kan ga roo

Letter–sound sequence

Focus: *hearing sounds in words*
articulating words slowly as a strategy to learn to read and spell

Make a number of cards with 2, 3 or 4 boxes drawn at the top of the cards. Alternatively, you could copy Blackline Master 5 on card and laminate for reuse. During shared and guided reading and writing show children how to first say the words slowly and later, slide each letter or letter cluster from the bottom of the card upwards into the appropriate box while at the same time articulating the words slowly.

Begin with single sounds and later move to blends and digraphs. (For more information about this procedure read Marie Clay's *Reading Recovery*: 'Hearing and recording sounds in words'.)

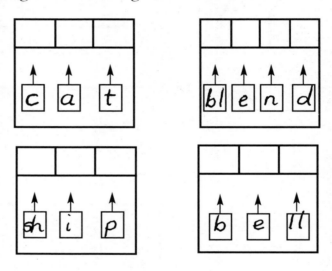

Bingo

• • • • •

Focus: *reinforce high-frequency words, initial blends, vowels, phrases and same-sound medial blends*

Make bingo cards with high-frequency words, initial blends, vowels, phrases and same-sound medial blends.

High-frequency words:

am	I	the
can	see	and

Playing Bingo with high-frequency words

Initial blends:

bl	cl	br
tr	sh	th

Vowel sounds:

p*i*g	l*e*t	m*a*t
h*u*t	p*o*t	s*i*t

Phrases:

I can	I am	we can
he can see	I am on	he went

The long /a/ sound ('ey' 'ai' 'ay'):

th*ey*	cl*ay*	m*ai*l	w*ay*	s*ai*l
tr*ai*l	r*ai*n	d*ay*	f*ai*nt	br*ai*n
s*ay*	gr*ey*	l*ay*	ch*ai*n	pr*ay*

Spelling pile

Focus: *independently practising spelling of words*

Each child in your class can have a 'pile' of spelling words to learn. The words can come from the topic being studied or from the child's writing. Put the 'pile' into an envelope with a flash-size card that has a 'happy face' and a 'to learn face' drawn on it. On the management task board, place a 'Spelling' card, separate from the 4 activity cards set for each group. Spelling could be a task children do each day before they begin their series of literacy activities.

Children get out their envelopes and check their own reading and spelling of words. When they read a word they turn it over and spell it to themselves. When they check that their spelling is correct they put it on the 'happy face' – the 'known pile'. If their spelling is incorrect or they cannot read the word they place it on the 'to learn face' – the 'unknown pile'. A child who may not be able to read some words is given a buddy to assist the reading of words only.

[known pile]　　[unknown pile

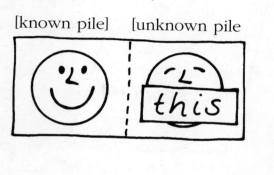

Activities stressing structure

Handwriting

Focus: *learning letters, word spacing and sentence order through handwriting*

Write the letters, word and sentence, into the children's handwriting book each week or put this pattern on laminated card for the children to copy.

One day a week, model the writing of a particular letter – capital and lower case, a word beginning with the letter, and a sentence. Show where to begin, and the spacing between words. Discuss the placement of capitals at the beginning of sentences and full stops at the end.

As a follow-up, the children practise writing the letters, word and sentence during literacy activity. Place a 'Handwriting' card on the management task board.

Copy short poems on card for children to write in their handwriting books, for example:

> i . . . .
> I . . . .
> **Incy Wincy spider**
> **Climbed up the water**
> **spout.**

Punctuation – quotation marks

Focus: *reinforcing knowledge*
practising using quotation marks

Read a big book which contains a lot of examples of direct speech (there are many to choose from). Begin with speech bubbles to focus on the spoken words only. Blu-tack speech bubbles on the big book pictures and write the direct speech from the text on them. This representation allows the children to see the direct speech only. Go back to the book and mask the writing, leaving only the direct speech visible.

As a follow-up during literacy activity have about ten sets of cards with a character on one card, perhaps asking a question (shown in a speech bubble) and a character on the other card answering (shown in a speech bubble). The children read and match the speech bubble cards.

Later, read another big book, for example *Yes Ma'am*, and extract the direct speech and write it on strips of card. Make separate quotation marks and colour them a different colour. In a class circle have children set out the direct speech cards and then put the 'talking marks' either side of the quotation.

Make a number of sets of different quotations and a enough quotation marks for children to manipulate during literacy activity. Later, add the verbs that indicate direct speech has occurred.

said the [   ].
answered the [   ].

4 Flying high

Activities for fluent readers

Activities stressing meaning

Word meanings

Focus: *word usage*
reinforcing the idea that a dictionary is a resource to extend knowledge of words, meanings and spelling
practising how to use a dictionary

After the group has read a novel, for example, choose words from it and have children find the meanings in a dictionary. Children can then write a sentence to show their understanding of the word.

You could also place cards or 'Post-it' notes in copies of the book.

Help yourself ... look in the dictionary

Look for a word that starts with _____ **and means** _____

Look for a word which tells how _____

Find this word _____ **in the dictionary and write what it means**

Homonyms

Focus: *reinforcing knowledge about homonyms, in this case, homographs*

Read books which have examples of homographs (words that are pronounced and spelt the same way but with different meanings). For example, there are wonderful examples of homographs in the stories about Amelia Bedelia. She is always very confused about meanings!

In *Amelia Bedelia and the Surprise Shower* Amelia is a maid and her employer is having a 'shower', a pre-wedding party for her friend Miss Alma. Amelia thinks shower relates to bathing. Amelia is again confused when Mr Rogers tells her to scale and ice some fish he has caught. She weighs the fish on the scales and puts cake icing on the fish. Amelia Bedelia stories are a fun way for children to learn about homographs.

During literacy activity, children look in dictionaries for two words that are spelt the same way, each having two different meanings.

Give children sets of coloured blank cards (blue for word, green for meaning). The children record the word and both the meanings. These cards could be displayed for 'read around the room' or references for further use (for example, writing amusing poems).

Semantic webs

Focus: *synthesising a story using key words or phrases*

A semantic web extracts the main ideas of a story or piece of information. Making semantic webs shows children how to plan using key words or phrases. Later, children use the web to rewrite the story (or information) using their own words.

Model a semantic web for a story, for example *The Magic Finger*. This is narrated by a girl who, when angry, is able to point her magic finger at people and turn them into animals. She dislikes hunting, and the Gregg family who are hunters are turned into ducks.

During literacy activity, children use this modelled web to rewrite the story in their own words.

When children can confidently use a web, they can use Blackline Master 6 to write the title and main points of a story they have read.

Charts and diagrams

Focus: *synthesising information from factual texts*
learning how information books often have diagrams as a way of visualising information

Begin by looking at diagrams of life cycles, for example frogs, in non-fiction texts and then demonstrate drawing a simple life cycle of a frog.

During literacy activity, children draw their own chart or diagram of the life cycle of a frog.

Later, examine other texts to see how other life cycles (for example butterflies) are represented. Children choose another life cycle and replicate it during literacy activity.

Non-fiction connection

Focus: *comparing similarities and differences in how information is presented*

With the children look at some non-fiction texts to examine and compare how they present information, for example: contents, pictures, diagrams, information, glossary.

During literacy activity, children chart and compare how information is presented in different books.

TITLE	CONTENTS	INFORMATION	DIAGRAMS	GLOSSARY
The Life of a Duck	*heading* *page numbers* *last page–* *facts*	*writing* *pictures* *headings*	*yes* *various*	*no (index, explanations in text)*
Look at Fur and Feathers				

Question-time

Focus: *children learning to ask themselves questions to solve problems*

After a group has finished reading a short novel, for example *A Bad Case of Magic*, devise a question map with the children.

Why is the title ....?
Does it tell me what the story is about?
Who was the main character?
Does it matter if it was a girl or boy?

Use the key words, for example *why, what, does* from the question map to make a large question dice. During literacy activity, the group takes turns to throw the dice while one member acts as a recorder. When a member of the group throws the dice and it shows 'Why' that member will generate a 'why' question about the text and the recorder will write it down. Approximately four questions could be created.

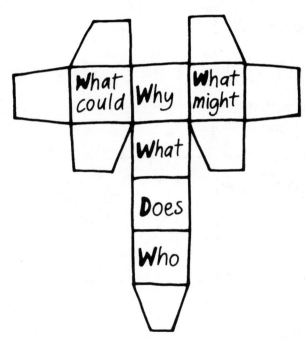

During the next literacy activity session, children can chose and answer one or two questions.

Designing a poster

Focus: *isolating the main point(s) about a story may involve language associated with advertising (for example, persuasive language)*

Children design a poster about a story they have read.

These could be displayed in a special area where other children can go to find out about books to read.

Jokes

• • • • •

Focus: *questions and answers*
reading a different genre
encouraging humour
contributing and sharing riddles and jokes

Write question and answer riddles. One way of presenting these is to cover cardboard cylinders (eg toilet rolls) with colored paper, write the riddles and answers on large white stickers, and stick these on cylinders. Encourage children to bring their favourite joke to school.

Put and take

· · · · · · · · · · · · · ·

Focus: *giving meaning-based descriptive instructions*
reinforcing knowledge about nouns (structure)

Demonstrate how to play this game for two players in a class circle. Each child has a board with the same words (nouns) or pictures.

lion	bike	house	hand
flower	truck	chair	elephant
ruler	clock	man	clown

They sit facing each other, and take turns to instruct their partner to 'put on' or 'take off' a counter by giving a meaning-based descriptive instruction. For example, rather than say: 'Put it on the lion,' they should say something like: 'Put it on the one that roars.' They need to remember whether they have instructed their opponent to put on or take off counters. The aim is to catch them out.

Child A: Put it on the one that roars.
Child B: Put it on the one with a trunk.
Child A: Put it on the one that walks on two legs.
Child B: Put it on the one that has an engine.
Child A: take it off the one that roars.
Child B: Put it on the one with a roof.
Child A: Put it on the one that measures.
Child B: Take it off the one that has a trunk.

Book reports

· · · · · · · · · · · · · ·

Focus: *retelling or summarising important aspects of a story*
simple analysis

During literacy activity, children reflect and report on a book they have read, using Blackline Master 7.

Another analytical approach in book reports can be children isolating, drawing or writing what the problem is in the story and stating or suggesting a solution.

Thinking hats

Focus: *practising the thinking stages required to make critical judgments and create ideas*

Use Edward de Bono's thinking hats strategies during shared reading. You can choose a big book or poem and decide what hat(s) would complement the book (de Bono's *Six Thinking Hats* suggests some books).

Make a chart of different coloured hats for children to refer to (there are templates for the hats in de Bono's book). Each hat defines a certain type of thinking:

red	feelings about the character and/or events
black	bad points – problems 'what is wrong?'
yellow	good points – why something works
white	facts
green	creative solutions – new or further ideas.
blue	plan / review – hats to use / what worked?

Design general task cards which refer to the most suitable hat(s). During literacy activity, children either respond to the big book or poem or read independently using the task card as a guide. For example, after a shared reading of *Postman Pete*:

Task: to design a new way Postman Pete could get around
Use the **blue** *hat to* write what the task is.
Use the **green** *hat to* design a different vehicle.
Use the **red** *hat to* say how you feel about the design.

After shared or guided reading:

Use the **white** *hat to list all the facts from the story.*

Use the **yellow** *and* **black** *hats to form and write an opinion about the character (or poem).*

First think of the
         good points   bad points

Opinion:

Use the **green** *hat to think / write a different ending*
or design a different cover
or draw 3 different settings.

How would your settings affect the story?

Use the **red** *hat to write how you felt about the story.*
How did the character feel?
How did you feel about the character?

CD-ROM comprehension work cards

Focus: *understanding the story.*

During shared reading, the class sits in front of the monitor and the complete story, for example *Arthur's Teacher Trouble* (Living Books), is played without interruption.

Make comprehension work cards for a particular group to complete. During literacy activity, the task will be for this group to replay part of the story and answer the questions. Limit the amount of pages the questions will cover. For example:

Arthur's Teacher Trouble

Page 6   What did the map of Africa look like to DW?

Page 7   What were the two cooking ingredients on Arthur's table?

Page 9   What were the ways different class members studied for the spell-a-thon?

Page 10   Where did Arthur like to study?

When the children know the story, ask more analytical questions – 'What if …?', 'How might …?'.

Activities stressing visual aspects

Compound words

Focus: *two words making another word*

Read a book which contains compound words, for example *bookworm* and *overcoat*.

In front of the children, represent an example of a compound word in pictures. Ask the children to look for more compound words in the story (or in dictionaries) and think about how they might represent the 'two words' in pictures.

During literacy activity, each member of a group finds two compound words in the dictionary and draws or writes the compound words. (Make the distinction between breaking words into syllables and compound words.)

Word searches and crosswords

Focus: *reading for meaning (meaning)*
          reinforcing verb knowledge (action words)

Read a story such as *More Spaghetti I Say*. From the text, extract a small number of verbs. Then use these to write clues and make a crossword grid.

During literacy activity, children first insert the missing verbs in the clues and then complete the crossword.

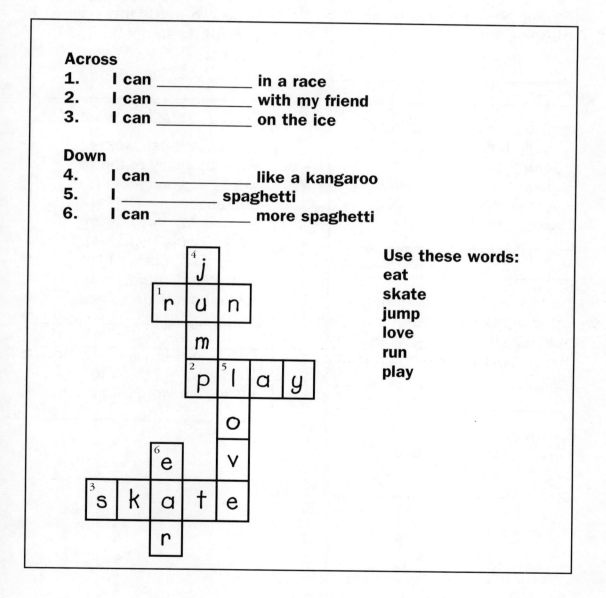

Across
1.   I can _____ in a race
2.   I can _____ with my friend
3.   I can _____ on the ice

Down
4.   I can _____ like a kangaroo
5.   I _____ spaghetti
6.   I can _____ more spaghetti

Use these words:
eat
skate
jump
love
run
play

Speed and accuracy

Focus: *varied – reinforcing homophones, prefixes, suffixes, digraphs, verb tenses*
quick mental response

This is a fun activity, and children love it. Make various cards which reinforce linguistic features. Have timers available and children complete as many cards as they can within a time limit. Spelling must be correct.

Write 20 words that begin with:
sh, ch, wh, th

Write two words that have each of these double vowels:
ea, ai, oa, oo, ee

Write words that sound like these but are spelled differently:
hear, too, there, blue, know, see, rode, ate, deer, maid

Add *er* to these words. Write as many of the *er* words as you can in one sentence.
fast, cold, new, warm, deep, soon, kind, bright, dark, fair, black, light, old, close, hard, clean, long, small, dear, near

Make word families from these endings:
ill, all, ound, ing, ake, et, ick, at, in

Use *p, r, c, m, f* to make new words from *an*

Write a word that begins with each of these letters:
g, k, w, n, s, l, m, p, b, r

CD-ROM language work cards

Focus: synonyms, spelling and word meanings

During shared reading of, for example, *Arthur's Teacher Trouble* (Living Books) demonstrate how to use language work cards that you have made.

During literacy activity, children in a particular group complete a language work card which relates to the text.

Arthur's Teacher Trouble

Look at the pictures on page 12. Find the 'faucet' and the 'pitcher'. What do we call these items? (*synonym*)

On page 20 a character incorrectly spelt a word that means frightened – 'feer'. How do you really spell that word? (*spelling*)

Use a dictionary to find the meaning of _____ _____. Make a sentence using the word _____ _____. (*word meaning*)

Activities stressing structure

Full stops, capitals

Focus: *knowledge of the sentence structure of full stops and capital letters*

After shared or guided reading, extract a short piece from the text and put it on laminated card. Omit the full stops and capital letters.

During literacy activity, children can rewrite the piece and insert the missing full stops and capital letters. They can check themselves by comparing their written piece with what is written in the book.

Capitals and full stops

it was a very good supper but there was so much of it he just sat back in his chair as full as he could be and decided he'd leave the dishes in the sink and do them the next night

but the next night he was twice as full and was twice as tired by the time he had finished so he left those dishes in the sink too

as the days went by there were so many dishes in the sink so he began to stack them on the table

(from *The Man Who Didn't Wash His Dishes*)

Later choose an extract from a story that includes both stops – full stops and question marks – and have children rewrite it, inserting the puctuation marks and capitals.

Categorising adjectives

Focus: *exposure to adjectives*

During shared reading, extract adjectives from texts. Categorise them under the headings: colour, size, feeling/mood, movement.

Make a laminated cardboard chart with columns and pockets. Write the words on card and during literacy activity the children can sort the descriptive words under headings.

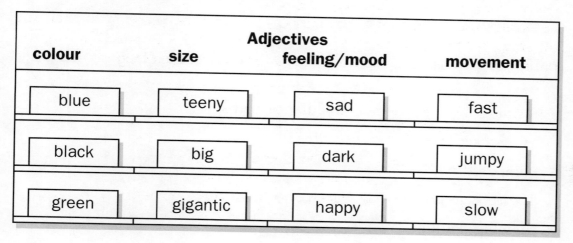

colour	size	**Adjectives** feeling/mood	movement
blue	teeny	sad	fast
black	big	dark	jumpy
green	gigantic	happy	slow

Have noun words, pictures or objects in a box, and during literacy activity a group could place an adjective from the chart in front of a noun. Another group could write poems using adjectives from the chart and nouns from the box.

Interesting sentences

Focus: *different sentence structures*

You can copy the Interesting Sentence grid on Blackline Master 8 onto a card, and laminate for reuse..

In big books, look for sentence structures that will help children's knowledge of language. For example:

- sentences using the noun/pronoun (singular and plural) structure

  Clyde likes to rock and roll. **He** said 'no' to other activities

  The **children** asked him to go down to the gym because **they** wanted him to have fun.

- forming the third person singular of verbs

  The **monkey jumps** from tree to tree.

  compared with

  The **monkeys jump** from tree to tree.

- rhyming within sentences

  Two **feet** walking in the **street**.

During shared reading, point out to the children the noun/pronoun usage, the rule for forming most third-person verb structures, and any other interesting structures. As you study each model, create more sentences for that model. During literacy activity, a group can order interesting sentences on the board.

Proper box

Focus: *grammar – tenses*

Keep a box with many laminated cards (numbered) so the children reinforce their grammar knowledge and use.

was   were
He _____ home early.
I wish you _____ here.

did   have done
You _____ that well.
You could _____ that better.

came   come
He _____very quickly when I called.
I will _____ to your party.

speak   spoke
I always _____ quietly.
They _____ to me yesterday

Spacing

Focus: *spacing between words*

For early readers, cut-up sentences are marvellous for assisting children's knowledge and use of spacing. Try this exercise for more experienced readers and writers.

Put the spaces between the words

Harrydoesn'tknowmuchabouthowwriting
works.Ifyouareabletoputinthespacingit
showsthatyouknowalotaboutwritingand
reading.

Blackline Master 1

Jigsaw letters

Blackline Master 2

Sequencing the alphabet

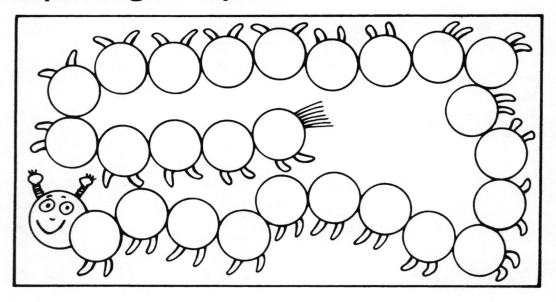
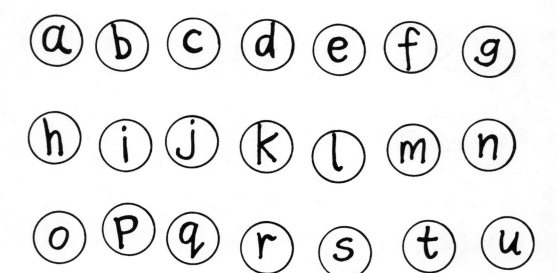

Blackline Master 3

True   *False*

Blackline Master 4

Book report

Date: Name:
My Book Report
The title:
The author:
Characters
Beginning
Events
Ending
The best part was ....
because

Blackline Master 5

Letter–sound sequences

Blackline Master 6

Semantic web

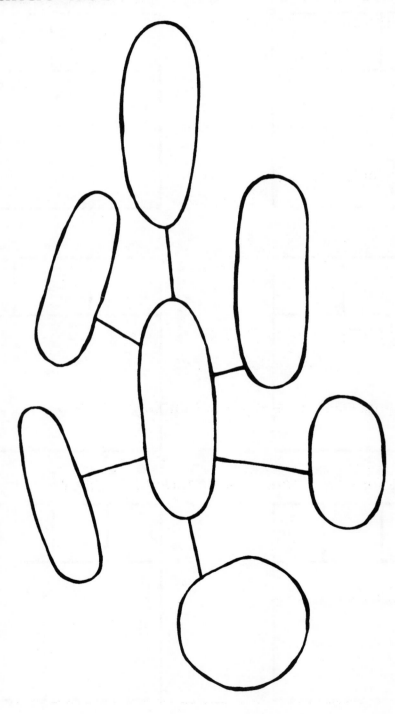

Blackline Master 7

Book report

Thinking about your story

Title

Who is the main character?

When/where did the story take place?

What did the main character do?

Could the character have done something different?

Could the story have been more interesting? Why?

Blackline Master 8

Interesting sentences

Bibliography

Alphakids, 1998. Horwitz Martin, Sydney.

Bonne, Rose 1981. *I Know an Old Lady*, (Scholastic Big Books). Ashton Scholastic, Gosford NSW.

Clay, Marie 1993. *Reading Recovery*. Heinemann Education, Auckland.

Croser, Josephine 1989. *The Life of a Duck*, (Magic Bean In-Fact Series). Era Publications, Adelaide.

Dahl, Roald, 1966. *The Magic Finger*. Penguin, Melbourne.

De Bono, Edward 1992. *Six Thinking Hats: Book 1*. Hawker Brownlow, Melbourne.

Faulkner, Keith 1995. *The Wide-mouthed Frog*. Koala Books, Sydney.

Fox, Mem 1983. *Possum Magic*. Omnibus Books, Adelaide.

Gelman, Rita Golden 1977. *More Spaghetti, I Say!* Scholastic, New York.

Holdaway, Don, 1979. Foundations of Literacy. Ashton Scholastic, Gosford NSW.

Hanzl, Anne 1986. *Silly Willy*. Ashton Scholastic, Gosford NSW.

Kitching, Katie & Wansborough, Chris 1996. *Storytime Topics*. Belair Publications,. London.

Krasilovsky, Phyllis 1950. *The Man Who Didn't Wash His Dishes*. Brøderbund, New York.

Living Books and Mercer Mayer CD-ROM. 1994. Random House, New York.

Mahy, Margaret 1997. *Guinea Pig Grass*. Rigby Heinemann, Melbourne.

Marshal, Val 1988. *Postman Pete*. Ashton Scholastic, Gosford NSW.

Melser, June 1989. *Smarty Pants*, (Read-together book). Shortland Publications, Auckland.

Melser, June 1980. *Yes Ma'am*. Shortland Publications, Auckland.

Oppel, Ken 1993. *A Bad Case of Magic*, (Young Puffin). Penguin, London.

Parish, Peggy 1977. *Amelia Bedelia*. World's Work Ltd. The Windmill Press, Tadworth, Surrey UK.

Parkes, Brenda 1989. *Goodnight, Goodnight*. Ginn & Co, Ontario.

Pascoe, Gwen 1976. *The Masked Hunter*. Era Publications, Adelaide.

Pluckrose, Henry 1989. *Look at Fur and Feathers*. Franklin Watts, London.

The PM Library Starters One, 1995. Nelson Price Milburn, Auckland.

Schaffer, Frank 1988. *Fairy Tale Sequencing: Visual Sequencing Cards,* Frank Schaffer Publications, Palo Verdes CA.

Scholastic Big Books 1981. *The Three Billy Goats Gruff*. Ashton Scholastic, Gosford NSW.

Thiele, Colin, 1963 'Storm Boy' Rigby Ltd. Adelaide

Tolstoy, A. & Oxenbury, Helen *The Great Big Enormous Turnip* 1972 Pan Books Ltd. London.